The NYSTR[...] Block Buddy ATLAS

Hi! We're the Block Buddies.
Come along with us . . .
. . . as we explore neighborhoods and maps.

HERFF JONES NYSTROM

Contents

A Picture Atlas of Neighborhoods 4–15

- Where do people live? 4–5
- What do neighborhoods look like? 6–7
- What are our needs and wants? 8–9
- Where do people work? 10–11
- What rules do people obey? 12–13
- How do neighborhoods change? 14–15

What Can You Learn About Maps and Globes? 16–27

- What view does a map show? 16–17
- How do maps show real places? 18–19
- What is a globe? 20–21
- How can you see the whole world at once? 22–23
- Where is your continent? 24–25
- How do maps show your country? 26–27

2012 Update of Names and Boundaries

4719 W. 62nd St., Indianapolis, Indiana 46268

Printed in U.S.A

10 9 8 7 6 16 15 14 13 12

Print ISBN: 978-0-7825-1022-5 Product Code: 9A97A
E-book ISBN: 978-0-7825-1597-8 Product Code: SL5-A97A-NA

To order: herffjonesnystrom.com or 800-621-8086

This list tells
what lies ahead!

Where Do You Live? 28–33

Where is your state? 28–29

What are symbols of our country? 30–31

What seasons does our capital have? 32–33

Looking At the Continents 34–45

How are other children in North America like you? 34–35

How are children in South America like you? 36–37

How are children in Africa like you? 38–39

How are children in Europe like you? 40–41

How are children in Asia like you? 42–43

How are these children like you? 44–45

Glossary 46–47

Index 48

Abbreviations inside back cover

Where do people live?

A Some people live in row houses.

B Others live in mobile homes.

C Some people live in big houses.

Some people in this neighborhood live in houses. Others live in apartments.

D Others live in apartment buildings.

What does YOUR home look like?

APARTMENTS
Factory
FOODS

E Some people live in farm houses.

F Others live in ranch houses.

G Many people live in small houses.

H Others live in high-rise condos.

What do neighborhoods

A Some neighborhoods have streets that curve.

B Others have straight streets.

This neighborhood has streets and buildings. So does yours.

look like?

APARTMENTS
Factory
FOODS
ALE 10¢

Which picture shows farms?

C Many neighborhoods have tall buildings.

D Some have houses close together.

How are these neighborhoods different?

E Others have houses far apart.

Are any of these like YOUR neighborhood?

What are our needs and

A We need ways to communicate with others.

This neighborhood has things people need. It also has things they want.

B We need food for our health.

C We need clothes to keep us warm.

wants?

D We need transportation for going places.

F We want toys for having fun.

E We need a place to live.

Where do people work?

A Bakers sell food at the bakery.

B Clerks put food on shelves at the grocery store.

Many places in this neighborhood are places to work.

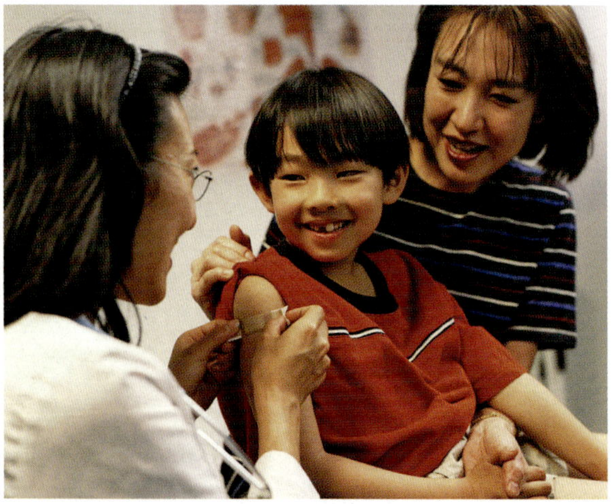

C Doctors work at the hospital and in offices.

APARTMENTS
Factory
FOODS

D Firefighters work at the firehouse and in the neighborhood.

E Cooks prepare food in restaurants.

F Some people work from home.

Where do people work in YOUR neighborhood?

What rules do people

We all follow rules in the neighborhood. Rules help keep us safe.

A Pet owners use leashes for walking their dogs.

B Students raise their hands to speak in class.

C Bike riders wear helmets.

obey?

APARTMENTS
Factory
FOODS

D Children recycle cans and paper.

What rules do you obey at home?

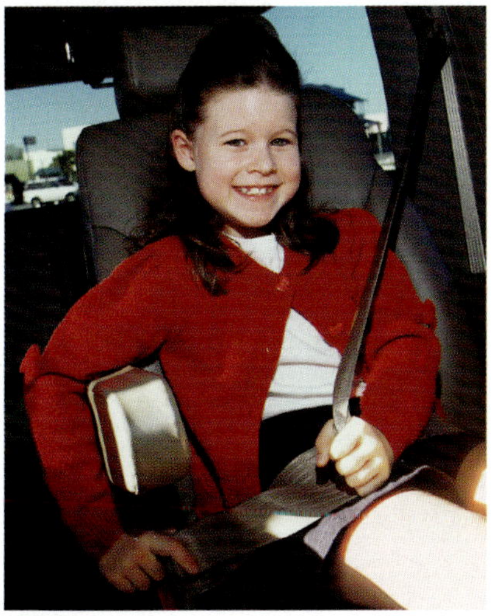

E Riders in cars wear seatbelts.

F People cross the street at crosswalks.

How do neighborhoods

A Long ago, only a few people lived here. Most of them lived on farms.

B More and more people came. They built new places to live, work, and learn.

change?

C Over the years the neighborhood kept changing. Today it looks like this.

D In the future, the neighborhood might look like this.

What view does a

A We see a **view from the ground** when we're walking.

We found this building in a park.

The same park is shown in all the pictures.

B A **bird's-eye view** looks down at an angle.

map show?

C A **view from directly above** looks straight down.

How is the map LIKE the photo?

How is the map DIFFERENT from the photo?

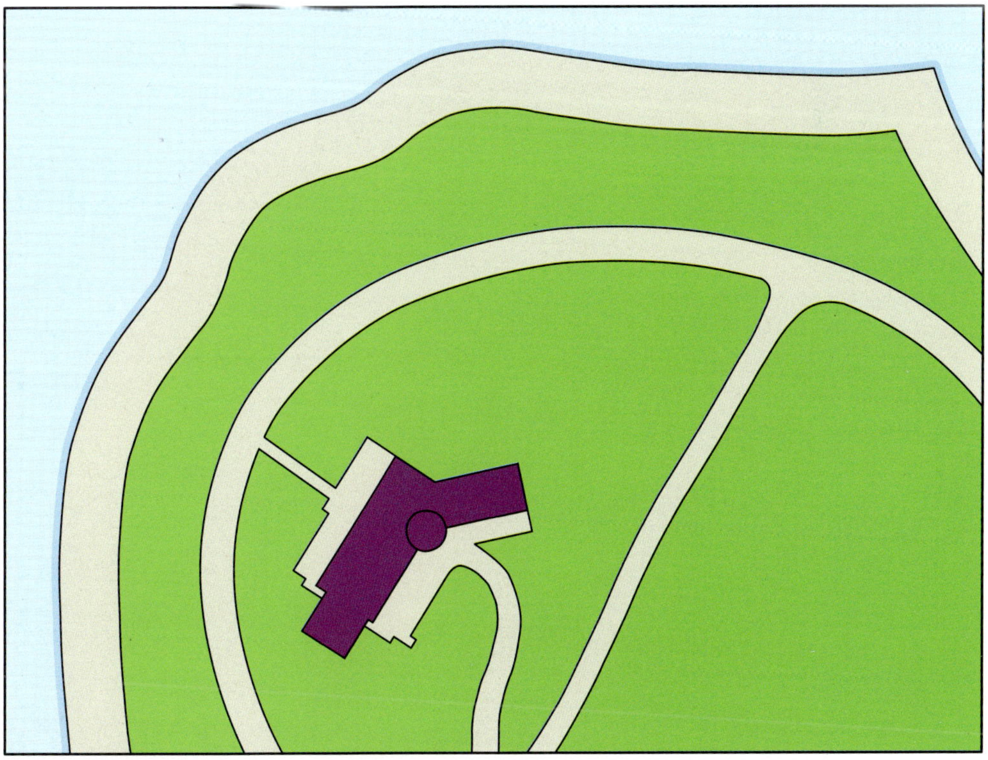

D A map is a special drawing of a view from directly above.

How do maps show

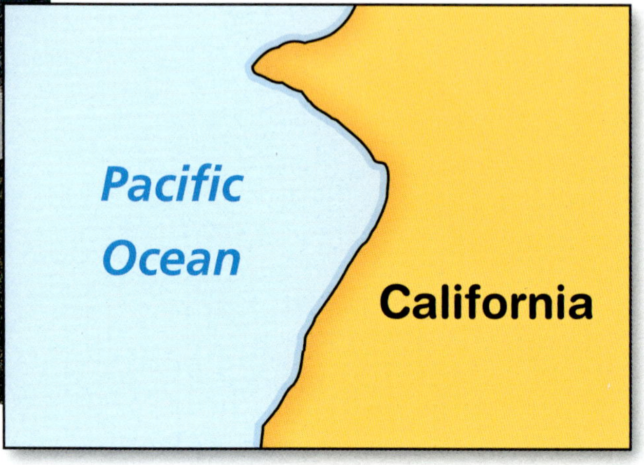

A A **coastline** is shown by a black line between land and water.

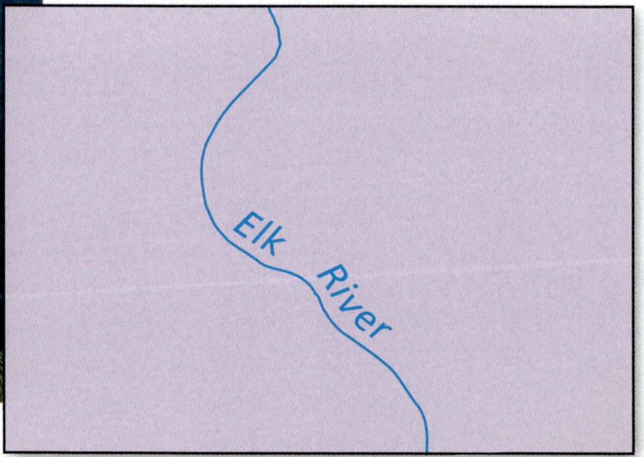

B A **river** is shown by a wavy blue line.

C A **lake** is shown by a blue area with land all around it.

real places?

D **Mountains** are shown by shadows.

E A **country capital** is shown by a red star in a circle.

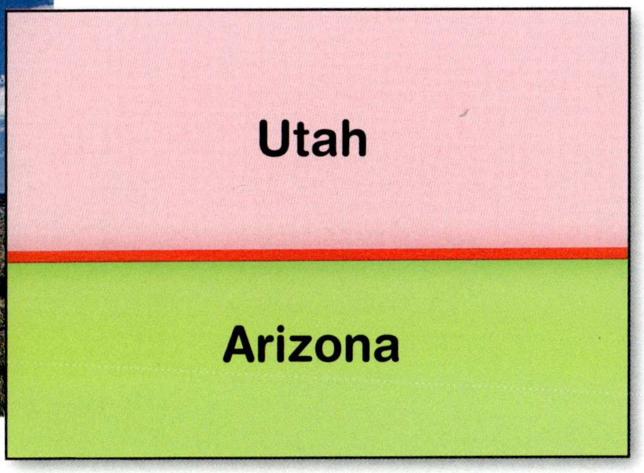

F A **boundary** is shown by a red line.

What is a globe?

Neighborhood Floor Map
NYSTROM

How is this model like the real thing?

A A globe is a model of the earth. This is a model of a neighborhood.

Some models look very real.

B This toy car is a model of a real car.

C The earth looks like this from space.

D Find ways this globe is like the earth.

How can you see the

A A globe shows one part of the world at a time.

B You see something new each time you turn a globe.

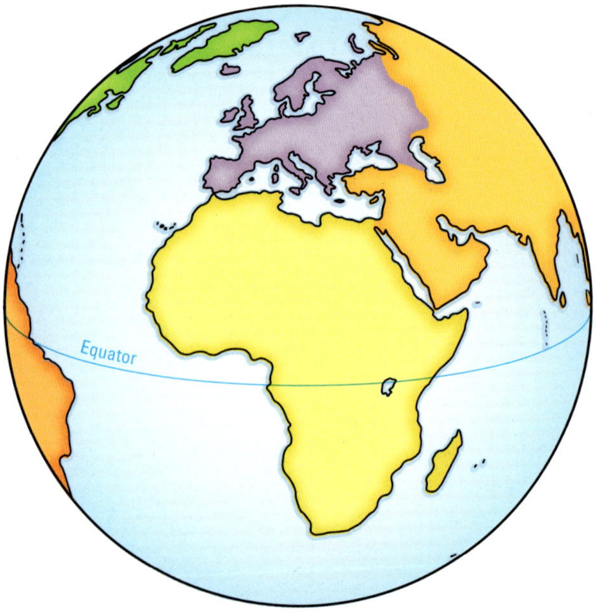

C Now you see another part of the world.

whole world at once?

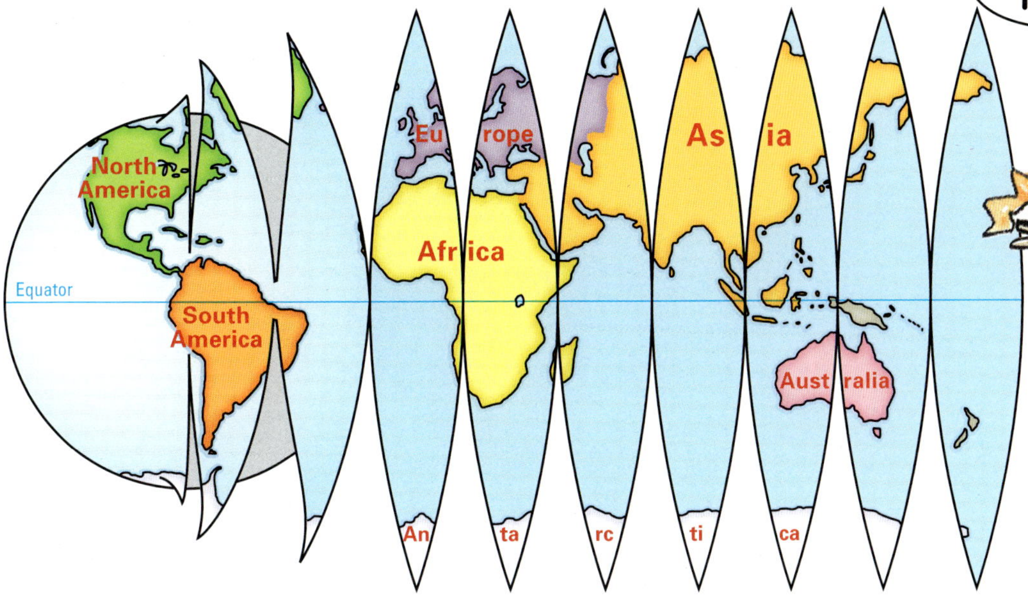

D Only a peeled globe can show the whole world at once.

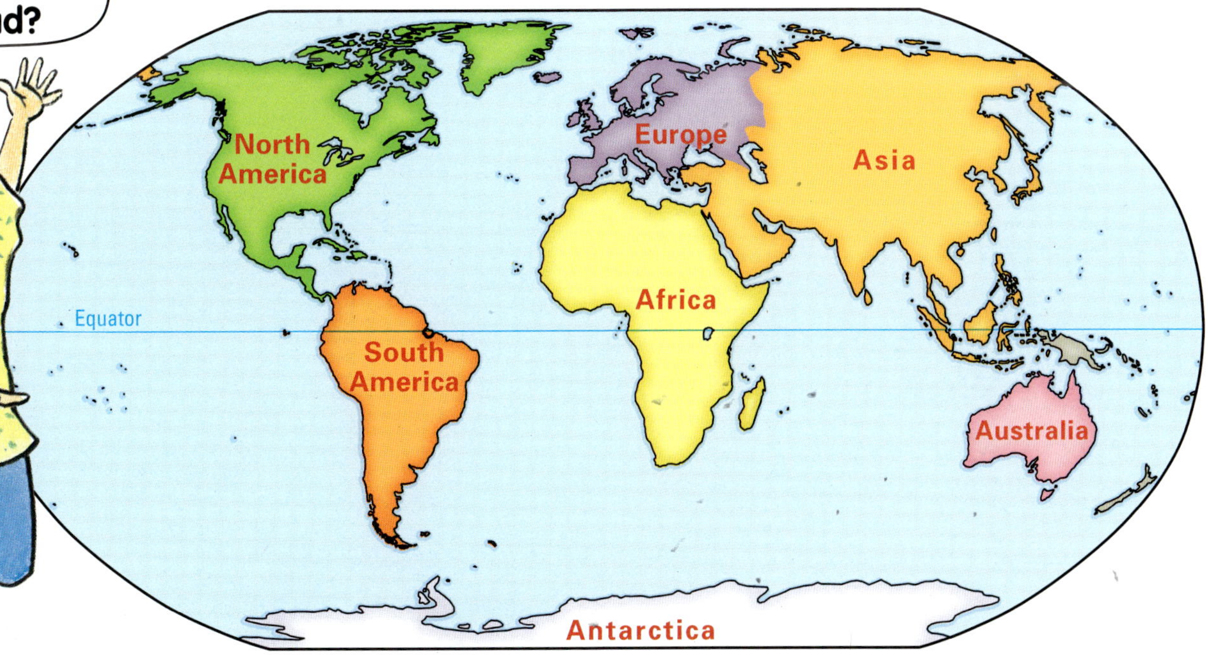

E A world map makes the whole world easy to see.

Where is your

continent?

Find the United States on this map.

The maps on page 27 will help you.

How do maps show your

Compare the
photo colors with
the map colors.

A Your country is outlined on this photo from outer space.

country?

B Continents are different colors on this map. Red lines show country boundaries.

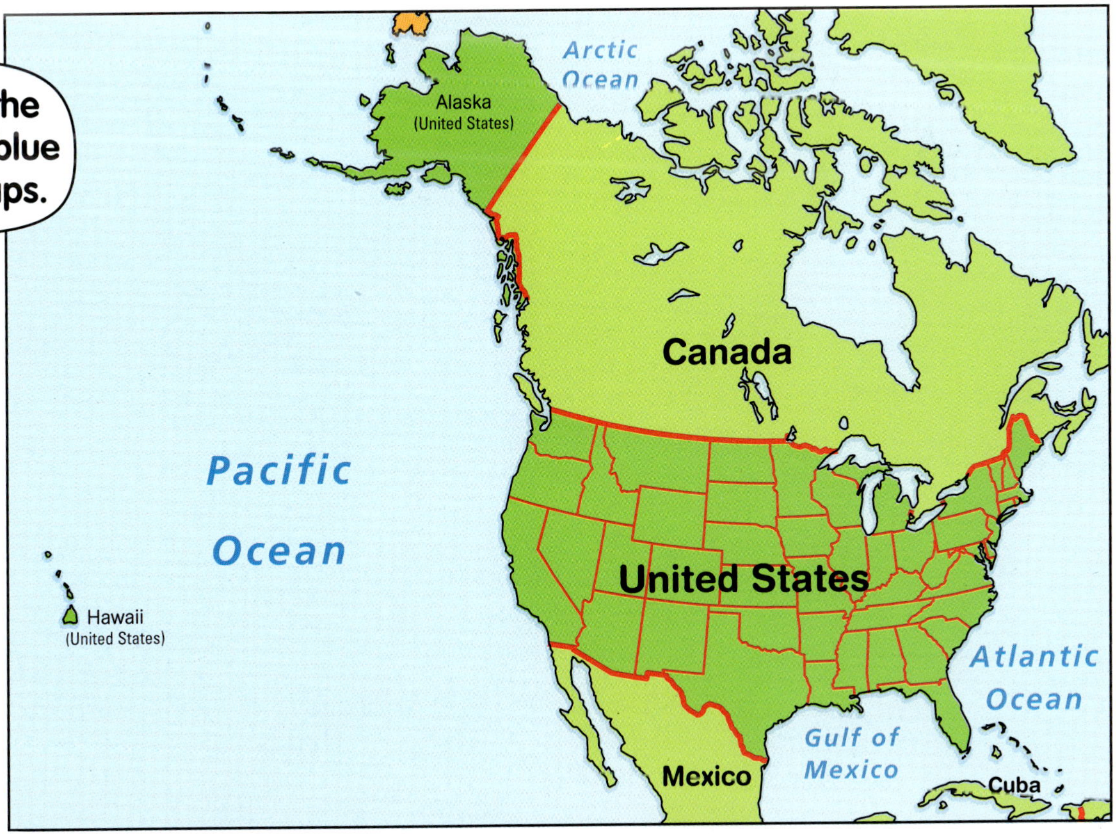

C Color makes your country stand out on this map. Red lines show state boundaries.

Where is your state?

Colors on this map show the states.
What color is yours?
nada
Lake Superior
Lake Michigan
Lake Huron
Lake Ontario
Lake Erie
Minnesota
Wisconsin
Michigan
Iowa
Illinois
Indiana
Ohio
Missouri
Kentucky
West Virginia
Virginia
Pennsylvania
New York
Vermont
New Hampshire
Maine
Massachusetts
Connecticut
Rhode Island
New Jersey
Washington, D.C.
Delaware
Maryland
North Carolina
South Carolina
Tennessee
Arkansas
s
oma
Mississippi
Alabama
Georgia
Louisiana
Florida
Atlantic Ocean
Gulf of Mexico
Cuba
N
W
E
S
United States
Mexico Country
Arizona State
Pacific Ocean Ocean, sea, gulf
Lake Michigan Lake
Washington, D.C. Country capital
Country boundary
State boundary
Mountains
Scale in miles
0 100 200 300 400
1 inch stands for 225 miles

What are symbols of

A Mount Rushmore honors four past U.S. presidents.

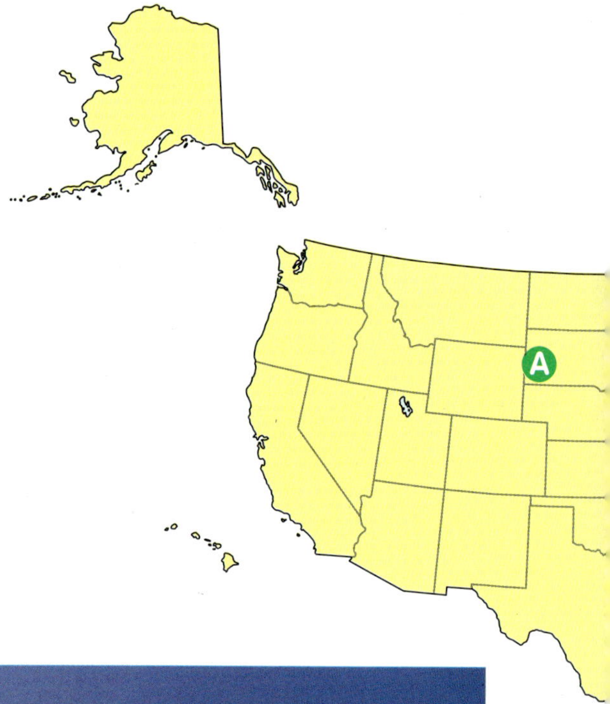
A

B This flag stands for the United States.

C The Statue of Liberty is a symbol of freedom.

Which of these symbols is in YOUR community?

our country?

You can find symbols of our country throughout the United States.

D The Capitol is where people meet to make our laws.

E The Liberty Bell celebrates independence.

F This memorial honors President Abraham Lincoln.

What seasons does our

Winter This is the coldest season. Water freezes and it may snow.

Washington, D.C. is the capital of the United States. Follow its cycle of seasons.

Fall Weather gets cooler. Leaves change color.

capital have?

Spring Weather gets warmer. Flowers and trees bloom.

Summer This is the hottest season. People can wear shorts.

How are other children in

Find North America in the world.

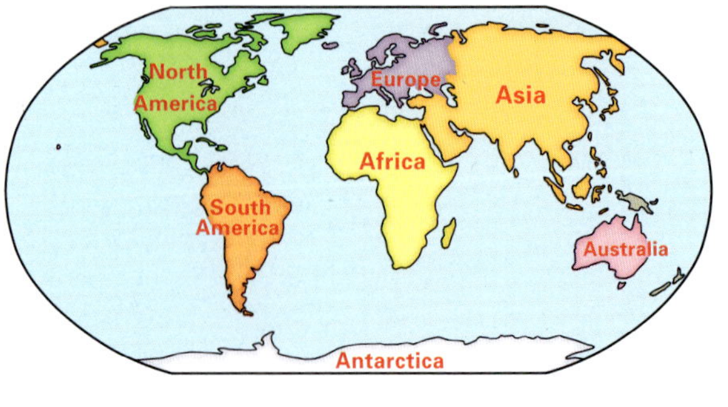

North America like you?

A Guatemala This boy waters plants for his family.

B Canada Children have fun in the snow.

C United States A family enjoys a picnic.

D Mexico Children play outside during recess.

E Trinidad and Tobago Children wear costumes for a holiday.

How are children in South

Name the continent that touches South America.

Find South America in the world.

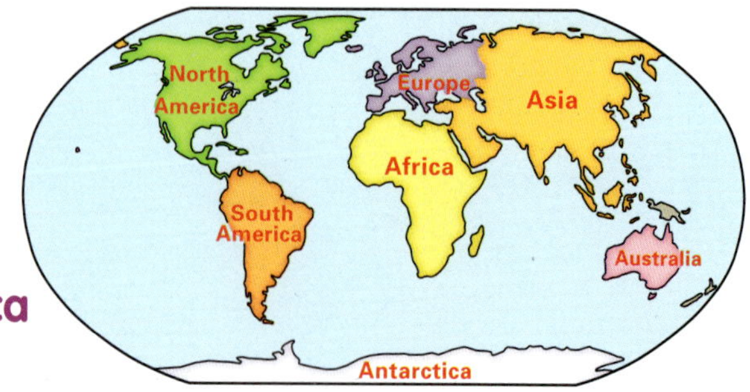

America like you?

A Venezuela Students learn to read.

B Brazil This boy plays at home.

Do you ever make things with your father?

C Peru Father and son work together.

D Bolivia This boy practices his music lesson.

E Argentina Children dance at a festival.

How are children in Africa

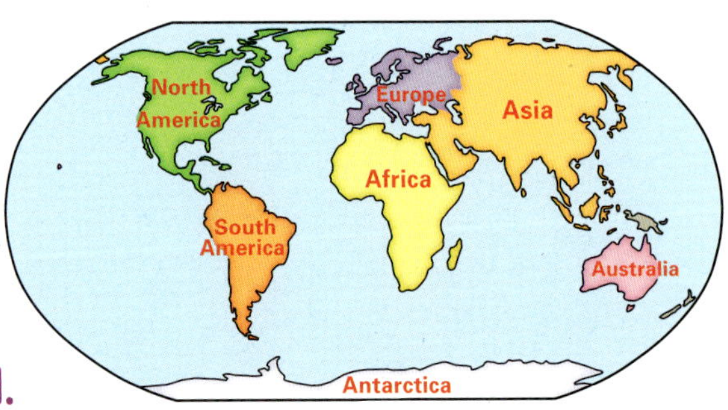

Find Africa in the world.

like you?

A **Equatorial Guinea**
A girl picks flowers.

B **Egypt** A father helps his daughter with her homework.

C **Kenya** Villagers hurry to a joyful celebration.

D **Togo** A girl carries her younger sister.

E **South Africa** Students work together in class.

How is YOUR schoolwork like this?

How are children in

A **Germany** A girl cuts out a picture.

B **Greece** A girl buys bread at the store.

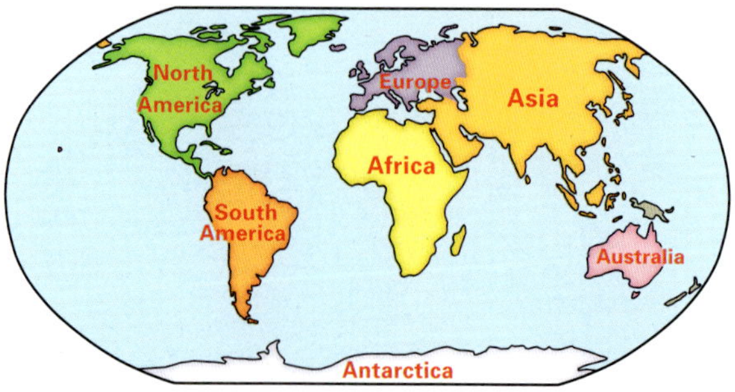

Find Europe in the world.

Europe like you?

C **Spain** This family enjoys a picnic.

D **Russia** Villagers celebrate Christmas.

E **Albania** Children play outside.

How are children in Asia

A **Israel** Children wear costumes on a holiday.

B **Japan** A family eats dinner together.

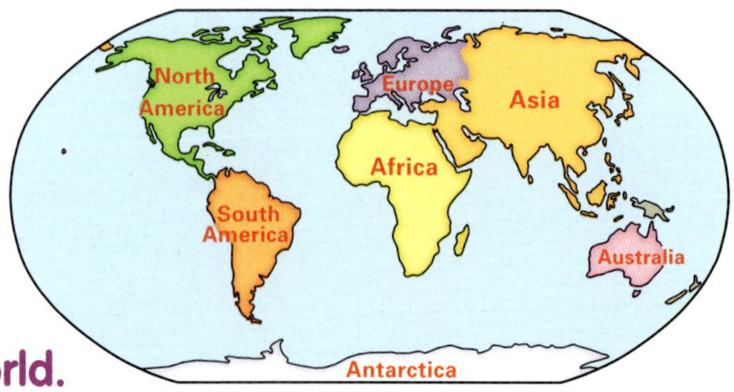

Find Asia in the world.

like you?

C **Indonesia** A boy carries coconuts for his mother.

D **Mongolia** Children tell funny jokes.

E **India** A girl practices her spelling.

How are these children

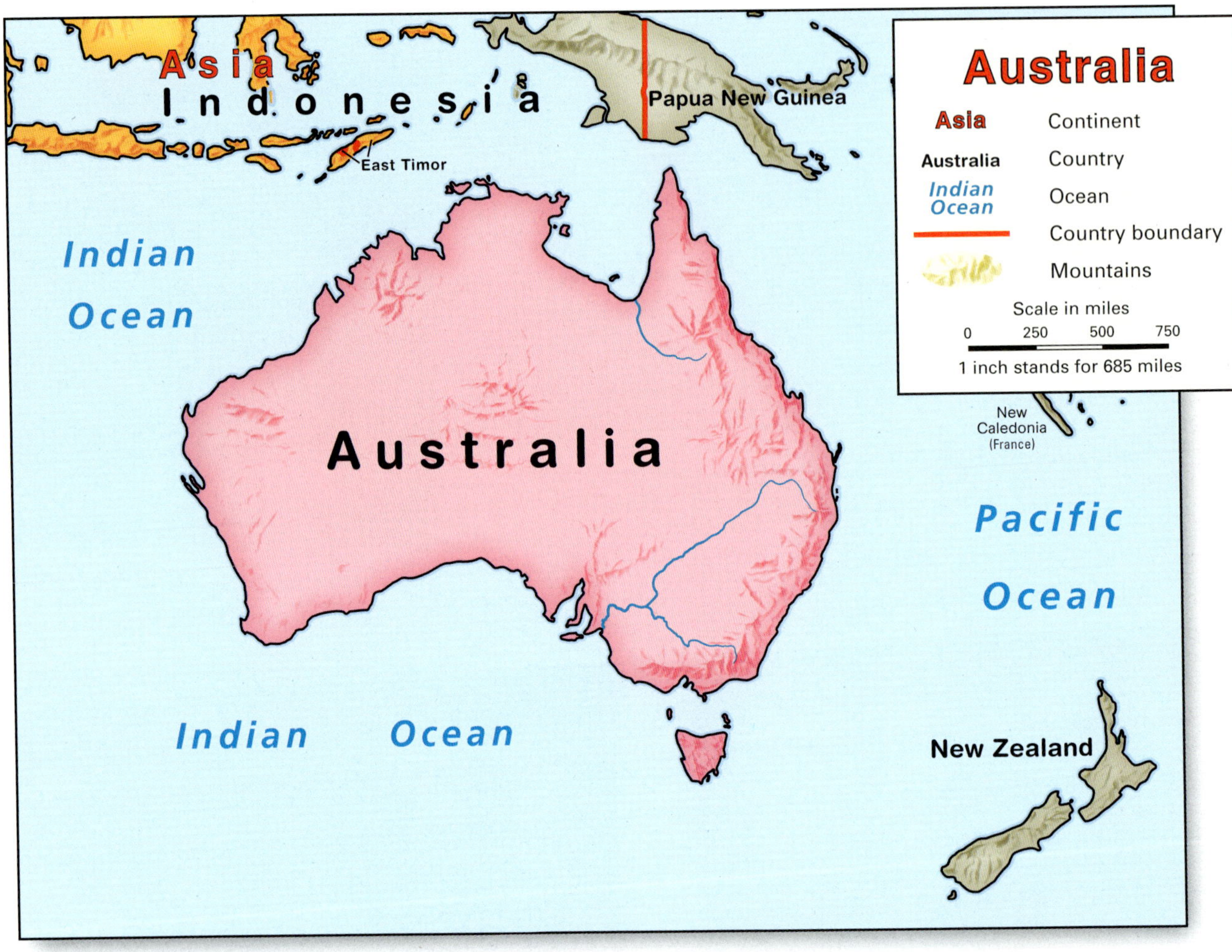

Find Australia in the world.

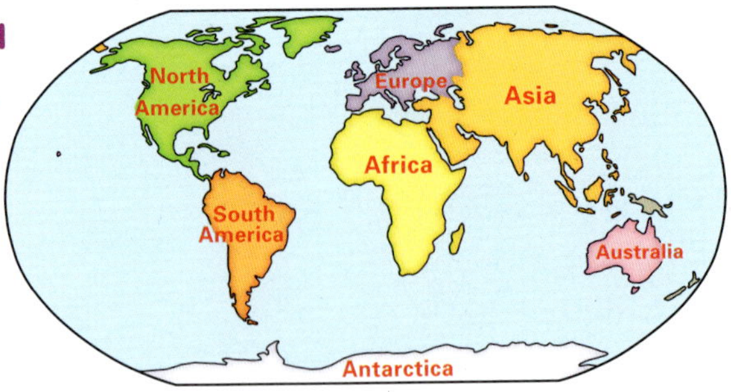

A Students listen to a story.

B A family enjoys its vacation.

like you?

Find Antarctica in the world.

C A penguin family stays warm.

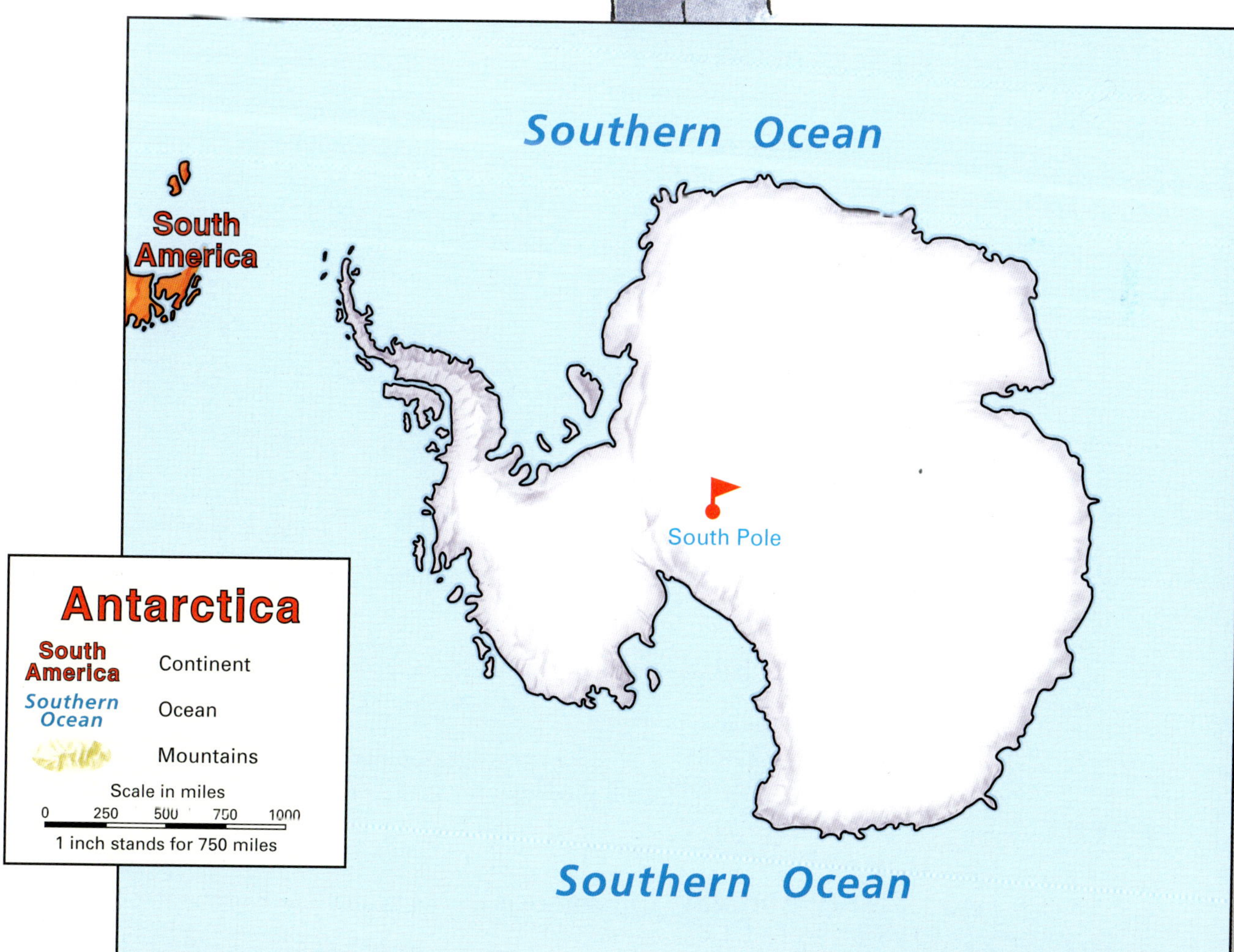

Glossary

atlas A book of maps.

boundary Where two states or countries meet.

capital City where the government of a country or state is located.

coastline The edge of a continent along a sea or an ocean.

continent One of the seven largest land areas on the earth.

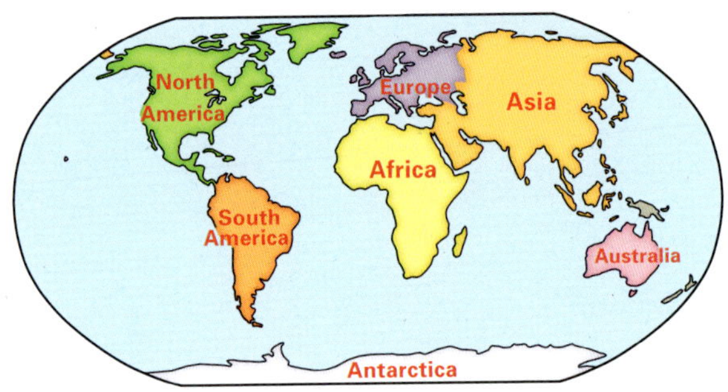

country A land with one government. Some countries have many states.

Equator Imaginary line around the middle of the earth.

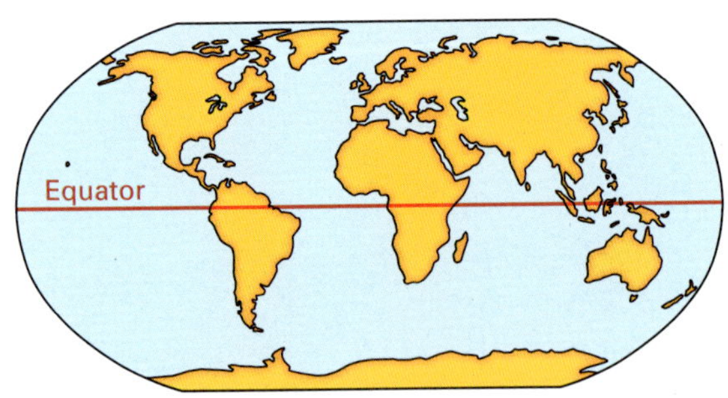

globe A model of the earth that is round like a ball.

island A body of land surrounded by water. An island is smaller than a continent.

lake A body of water, usually fresh. The water in a lake stays in one place.

map A special drawing of all or part of the earth as seen from directly above.

model A copy of an object, often smaller than the real thing.

mountain Part of the earth that is much taller than the land around it.

needs Things that make it possible to live.

neighborhood An area where people live.

ocean One of the five large bodies of salt water that cover most of the earth.

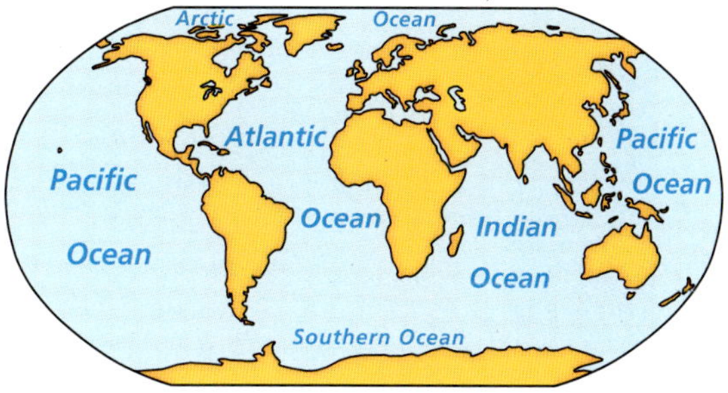

river A long, narrow body of water. The water in a river flows downhill.

rule Statement that tells what to do or what not to do.

season A part of the year that is hotter or colder than the part of the year that came before. The four seasons are winter, spring, summer, and fall.

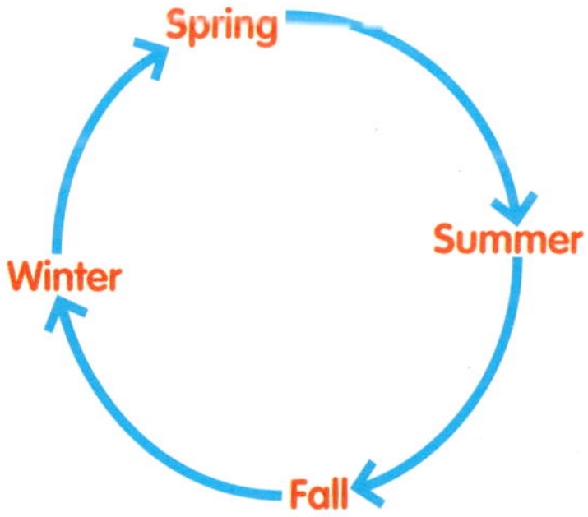

state Part of a country. There are 50 states in the United States of America.

symbol Line, shape, color, or object that stands for something else.

view What can be seen from a certain place, looking in a certain direction.

wants Things that make life more fun.

Index

Find
countries
here!

A-B-C

Afghanistan , *Asia* 42
Albania, *Europe* 40
Algeria, *Africa* 38
Angola, *Africa* 38
Argentina, *South America* 36
Armenia, *Asia* 42
Australia, *Indian Ocean* 44
Austria, *Europe* 40
Bahamas, *Atlantic Ocean* 34
Bangladesh, *Asia* 42
Belarus, *Europe* 41
Belgium, *Europe* 40
Bolivia, *South America* 36
Bosnia-Herzegovina, *Europe* 40
Botswana, *Africa* 38
Brazil, *South America* 36
Bulgaria, *Europe* 40–41
Burkina Faso, *Africa* 38
Burundi, *Africa* 38
Cambodia, *Asia* 43
Cameroon, *Africa* 38
Canada, *North America* 34
Central African Republic, *Africa* 38
Chad, *Africa* 38
Chile, *South America* 36
China, *Asia* 42–43
Colombia, *South America* 36
Congo Republic, *Africa* 38
Costa Rica, *North America* 34
Côte d'Ivoire, *Africa* 38
Croatia, *Europe* 40
Cuba, *Caribbean Sea* 34
Czech Republic, *Europe* 40

D-E-F

Democratic Republic of the Congo, *Africa* 38
Denmark, *Europe* 40
Djibouti, *Africa* 38
Dominican Republic, *Caribbean Sea* 34
East Timor, *Asia* 43
Ecuador, *South America* 36
Egypt, *Africa and Asia* 38
El Salvador, *North America* 34
Eritrea, *Africa* 38
Estonia, *Europe* 41
Ethiopia, *Africa* 38
Finland, *Europe* 40–41
France, *Europe* 40

G-H-I

Gabon, *Africa* 38
Gambia, *Africa* 38
Georgia, *Asia and Europe* 42
Germany, *Europe* 40
Ghana, *Africa* 38
Greece, *Europe* 40–41
Guatemala, *North America* 34
Guinea, *Africa* 38
Guyana, *South America* 36
Haiti, *Caribbean Sea* 34
Honduras, *North America* 34
Hungary, *Europe* 40
Iceland, *Atlantic Ocean* 40
India, *Asia* 42–43
Indonesia, *Asia* 43
Iran, *Asia* 42
Iraq, *Asia* 42
Ireland, *Europe* 40
Israel, *Asia* 42
Italy, *Europe* 40

J-K-L

Jamaica, *Caribbean Sea* 34
Japan, *Asia* 43
Jordan, *Asia* 42
Kazakhstan, *Asia and Europe* 42
Kenya, *Africa* 38
Kosovo, *Europe* 40
Kuwait, *Asia* 42
Laos, *Asia* 43
Lebanon, *Asia* 42
Latvia, *Europe* 40–41
Liberia, *Africa* 38
Libya, *Africa* 38
Lithuania, *Europe* 40–41

M-N-O

Macedonia, *Europe* 40
Madagascar, *Africa* 38
Malawi, *Africa* 38
Malaysia, *Asia* 43
Mali, *Africa* 38
Mauritania, *Africa* 38
Mexico, *North America* 34
Moldova, *Europe* 41
Mongolia, *Asia* 42–43
Montenegro, *Europe* 40
Morocco, *Africa* 38
Mozambique, *Africa* 38
Myanmar, *Asia* 42–43
Namibia, *Africa* 38
Nepal, *Asia* 42
Netherlands, *Europe* 40
New Zealand, *Pacific Ocean* 44
Nicaragua, *North America* 34
Niger, *Africa* 38
Nigeria, *Africa* 38
North Korea, *Asia* 43
Norway, *Europe* 40–41
Oman, *Asia* 42

P-Q-R

Pakistan, *Asia* 42
Panama, *North America* 34
Papua New Guinea, *Pacific Ocean* 44
Paraguay, *South America* 36
Peru, *South America* 36
Philippines, *Asia* 43
Poland, *Europe* 40–41
Portugal, *Europe* 40
Qatar, *Asia* 42
Romania, *Europe* 40–41
Russia, *Europe and Asia* 40–43
Rwanda, *Africa* 38

S-T-U

Saudi Arabia, *Asia* 42
Senegal, *Africa* 38
Serbia, *Europe* 40
Sierra Leone, *Africa* 38
Singapore, *Asia* 43
Slovakia, *Europe* 40
Slovenia, *Europe* 40
Somalia, *Africa* 38
South Africa, *Africa* 38
South Korea, *Asia* 43
South Sudan, *Africa* 38
Spain, *Europe* 40
Sri Lanka, *Asia* 42
Sudan, *Africa* 38
Sweden, *Europe* 40–41
Switzerland, *Europe* 40
Syria, *Asia* 42
Taiwan, *Asia* 43
Tanzania, *Africa* 38
Thailand, *Asia* 43
Tunisia, *Africa* 38
Turkey, *Asia and Europe* 42
Turkmenistan, *Asia* 42
Uganda, *Africa* 38
Ukraine, *Europe* 40–41
United Kingdom, *Europe* 40
United States, *North America* 28–29
Uruguay, *South America* 36
Uzbekistan, *Asia* 42

V-W-X-Y-Z

Venezuela, *South America* 36
Vietnam, *Asia* 43
Yemen, *Asia* 42
Zambia, *Africa* 38
Zimbabwe, *Africa* 38